Mama,
I Just Want to Be
LOVED

PAGE PUBLISHING
Conneaut Lake, PA

First originally published by Page Publishing 2024

ISBN 979-8-88654-176-2 (pbk)
ISBN 979-8-88654-182-3 (digital)

Printed in the United States of America

Mama,
I Just Want to Be
LOVED

Andrea Hill

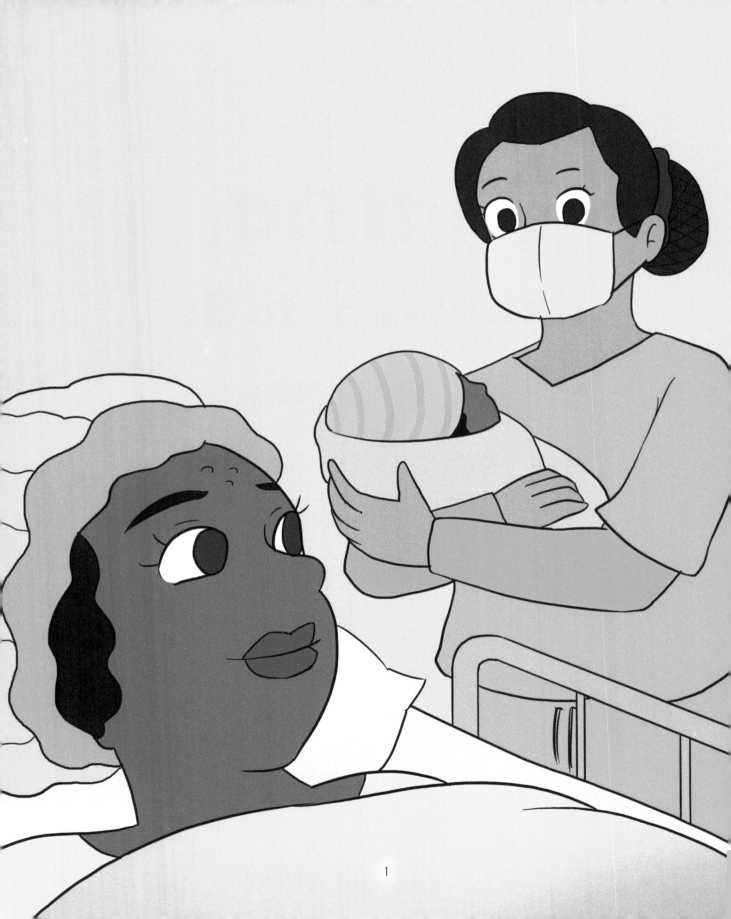

When I was born, I was the apple of my mom's eye. Although I was a girl, I looked just like a guy, that guy being my dad. "A splitting image," they said, "with a head full of hair and a smile that would light up like a sunshine ray."

My mom would hold me in the cradle of her arms, and all the other people would be drawn in by my charm. I was a happy and loved little one with no worries, just lots of fun, fun, fun.

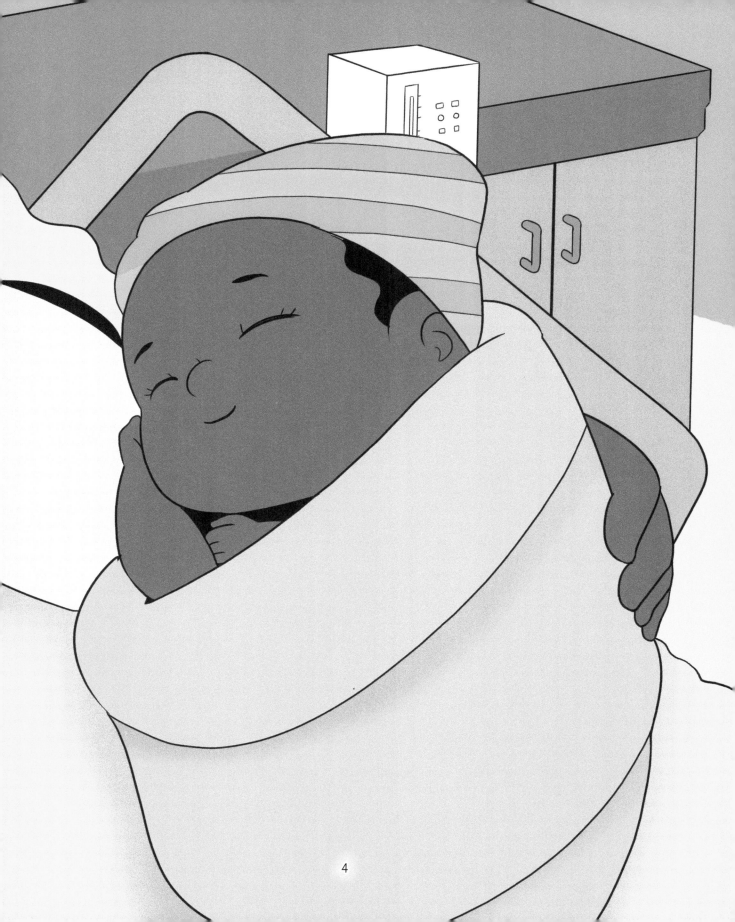

4

Everything was fine with Mommy and me until I started seeing her with a growing belly. Mom then told me that I would be a big sister soon. Although I didn't fully understand, I was as happy as when I heard the cow jumped over the moon.

The day finally arrived that I would see what kind of a big sister I would be. I went to the hospital with Ganny-Ma and Dan-Dan (my grandmother and grandfather) with a funny feeling as I held their hands. I went to the door, and what I did see in my mom's arms was a littler person who favored me.

She was much smaller and squiggly too. I was now a big sister but still didn't know what to do. I was now a big sister to a little sister, and she would be my friend. I would look out for and take care of her to the end.

That's what I thought I would do, but as she got older, I seemed to fade out of view. Mom was more caring to her needs, and I felt like nothing but an old dried-up weed. There was a little attention that I received, but it was always overshadowed by what my little sister achieved. I was lonely even if the room was full of people all around. Invisible I was, and therefore, I could not be found.

I acted out as much as I could so that at least they would hear my sound. You see, it was hard for me to understand that as a big sister, you had to be your little sister's biggest fan.

My head-start and pre-K teachers wondered what to do. Why was I acting out and feeling so blue? Finally, I told my pre-K teacher as tears fell down my cheeks like a flood. I just wanted to be loved. She looked so caringly at my face and wiped my tears at a slow, heartfelt pace.

16

Granny–Ma came, and the message of what I had said was told. She wrapped her arms around me in a loving hold. She talked to me about love and what it meant. She even told me how it might seem.

I was able to go to my mom and say as sincere as a dove, "Mama, I just want to be loved." The look in her eye was of pure shock, for she never wanted me to feel like an old sock. She hugged me and held me like she did when I was small. And she said that she loved me, would always love me, and would never let me fall.

That day was one of the best days that I can remember. Well, that is until I got all my presents in December.

Now I am a big sister who knows that she is loved, and I will show that to my little sister because that's what a big sister does!

The End

About the Author

Andrea Hill is a teacher, poet, and writer of various works. She is married and has two children and three grandchildren: two girls and a baby boy who is fourteen months old. In her spare time, she loves to cook, write, and make delicious, decorated cakes. The loving character that she plays is that of a sister that spreads the love, and she leaves some of her love everywhere she goes. Her passion for helping others is her focus, and this has afforded her to visit numerous places and encounter hundreds of people along the way. This story, *Mama, I Just Want to Be Loved*, comes out of that love that she has for her granddaughters. And she hopes that it helps other siblings dealing with the arrival of another person who needs Mama's attention.

Printed in the USA
CPSIA information can be obtained
at www.ICGtesting.com
CBHW060336041024
15321CB00075B/3992